HAL•LEONARD
INSTRUMENTAL
PLAY-ALONG

MW01526142

12 SMASH HITS

THE CD IS PLAYABLE ON ANY CD PLAYER, AND IS ALSO ENHANCED
SO MAC AND PC USERS CAN ADJUST THE RECORDING TO ANY TEMPO
WITHOUT CHANGING THE PITCH!

ISBN 978-1-4803-4119-7

HAL•LEONARD®
CORPORATION

7777 W. BLUEMOUND RD. P.O. BOX 13819 MILWAUKEE, WI 53213

Visit Hal Leonard Online at
www.halleonard.com

CONTENTS

THE A TEAM

1/2

ALTO SAX

Words and Music by
ED SHEERAN

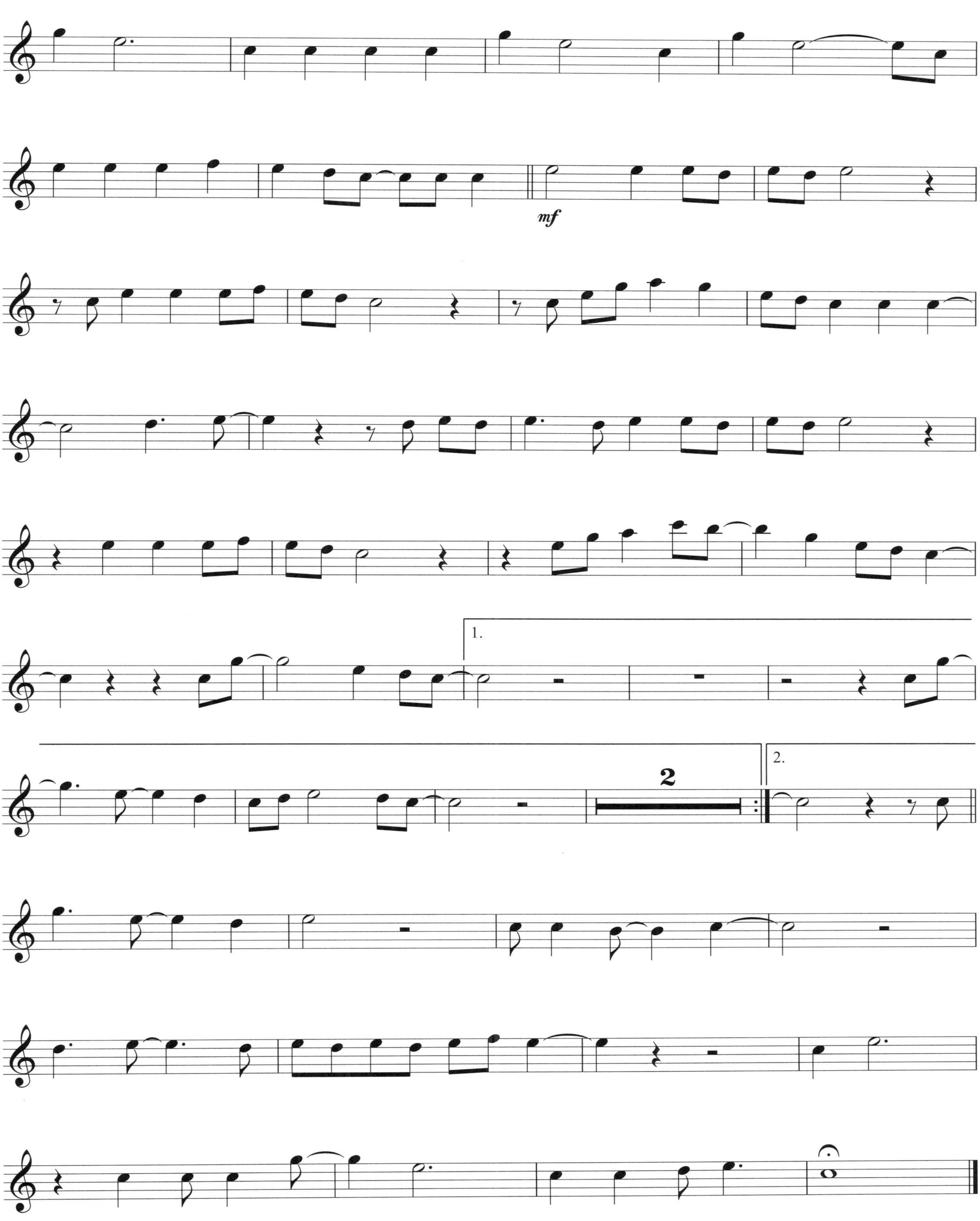
mf
1.
2
2.

GOOD TIME

3/4

ALTO SAX

Words and Music by ADAM YOUNG,
MATTHEW THIESSEN and BRIAN LEE

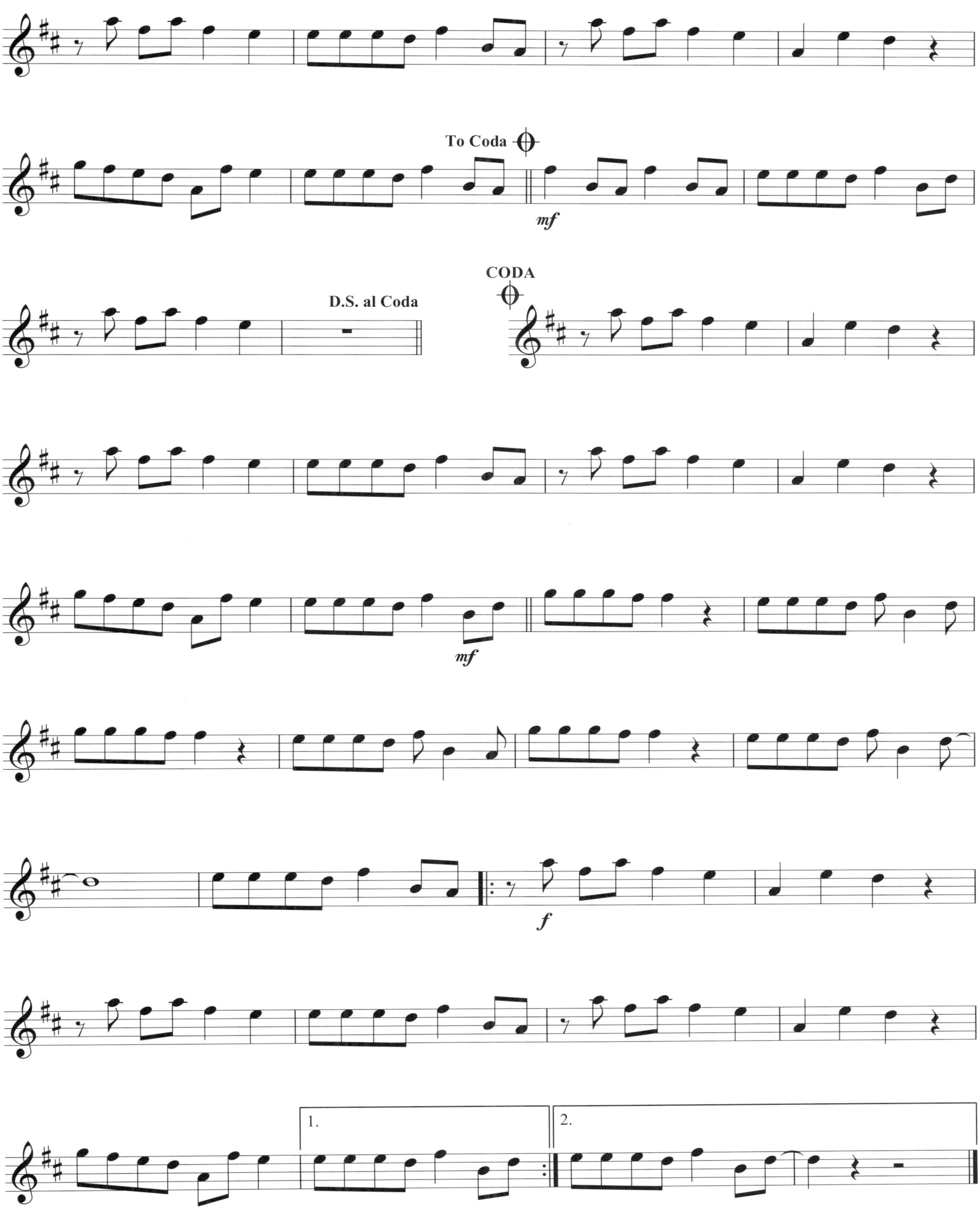
To Coda
mf
D.S. al Coda
CODA
mf
f
1.
2.

HO HEY

5/6

ALTO SAX

Words and Music by JEREMY FRAITES
and WESLEY SCHULTZ

Moderately

Guitar

Play

mf

4

f

8

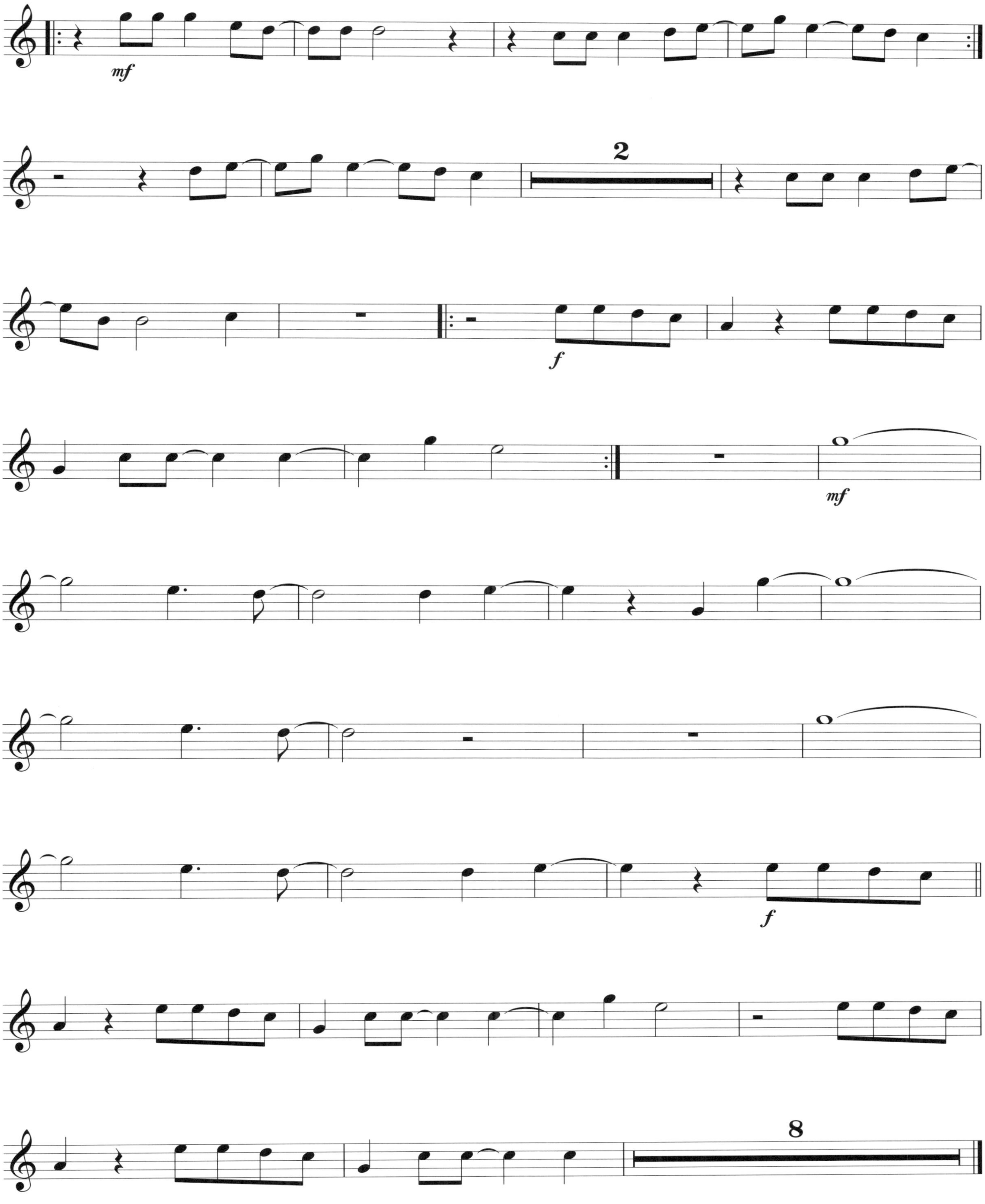
mf
2
f
mf
f
8

HOME

7/8

ALTO SAX

Words and Music by GREG HOLDEN
and DREW PEARSON

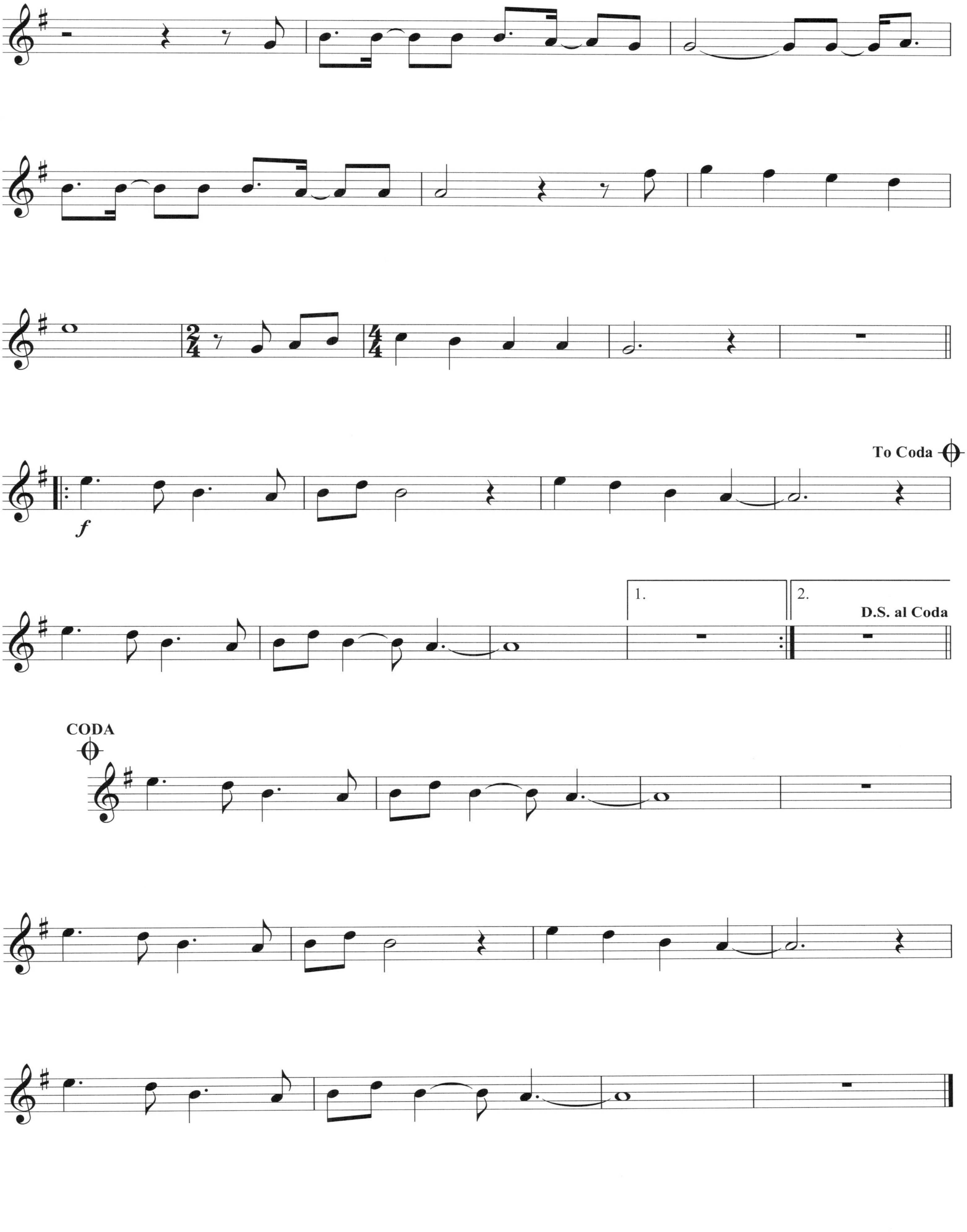

To Coda
1.
2.
D.S. al Coda
CODA

I KNEW YOU WERE TROUBLE.

ALTO SAX

Words and Music by TAYLOR SWIFT,
SHELLBACK and MAX MARTIN

IT'S TIME

ALTO SAX

Words and Music by DANIEL REYNOLDS,
BENJAMIN McKEE and DANIEL SERMON

LIVE WHILE WE'RE YOUNG

13/14
ALTO SAX

Words and Music by RAMI YACOUB,
SAVAN KOTECHA and CARL FALK

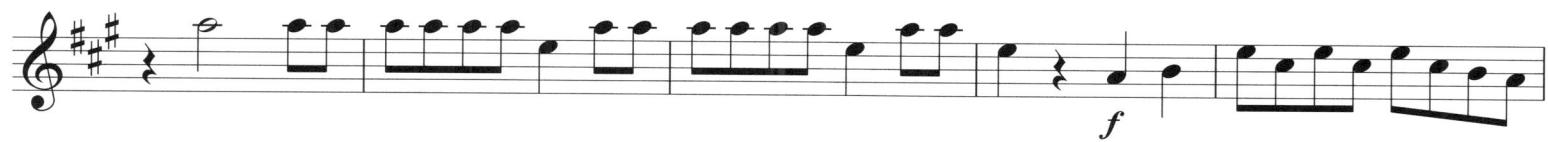

SKYFALL

from the Motion Picture SKYFALL

ALTO SAX

Words and Music by ADELE ADKINS
and PAUL EPWORTH

Slowly, with feeling

TOO CLOSE

17/18

ALTO SAX

Words and Music by ALEX CLAIRE
and JIM DUGUID

SOME NIGHTS

19/20

ALTO SAX

Words and Music by JEFF BHASKER,
ANDREW DOST, JACK ANTONOFF
and NATE RUESS

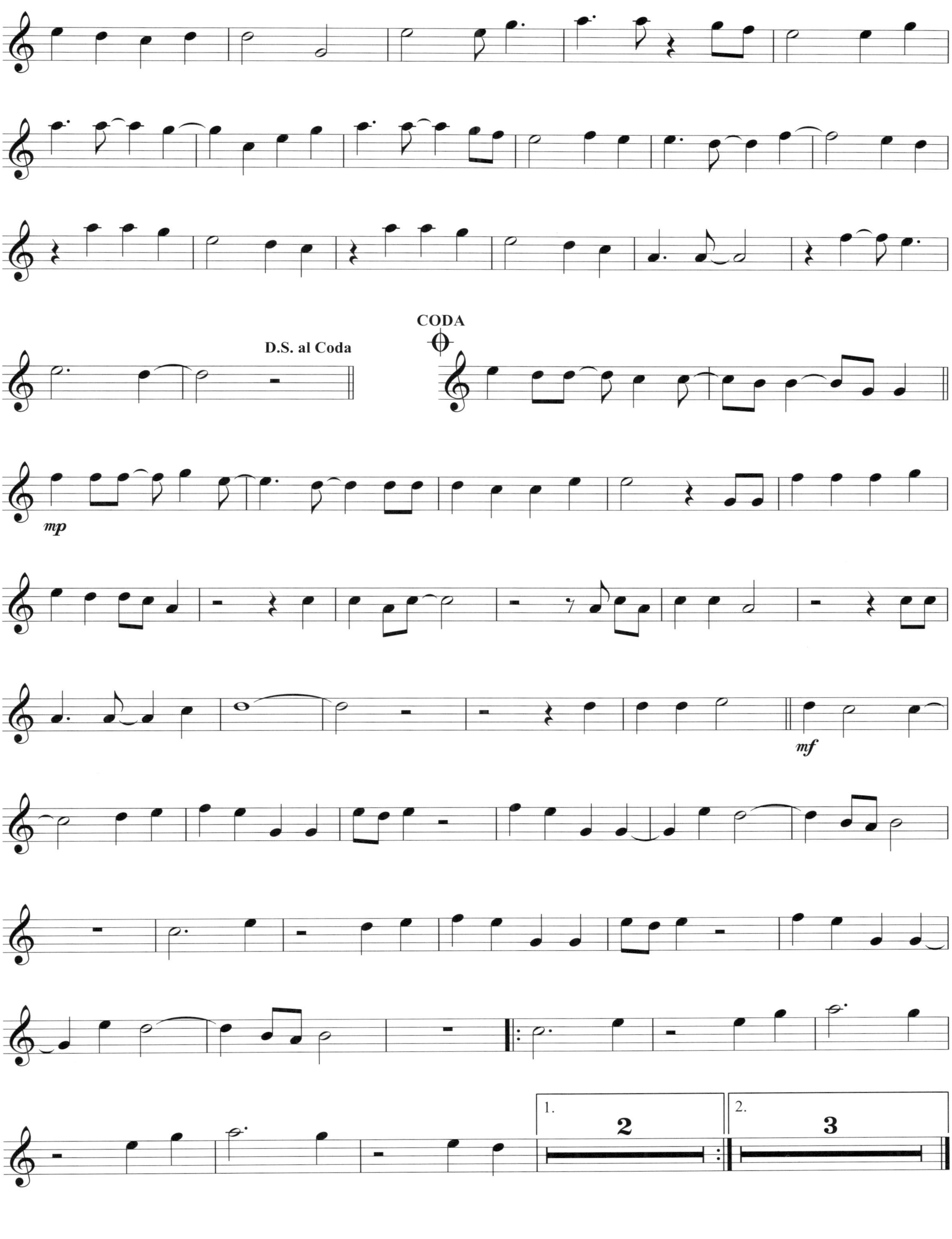
D.S. al Coda
CODA
mp
mf
1.
2
2.
3

STRONGER
(What Doesn't Kill You)

ALTO SAX

Words and Music by GREG KURSTIN,
JORGEN ELOFSSON, DAVID GAMSON
and ALEXANDRA TAMPOSI

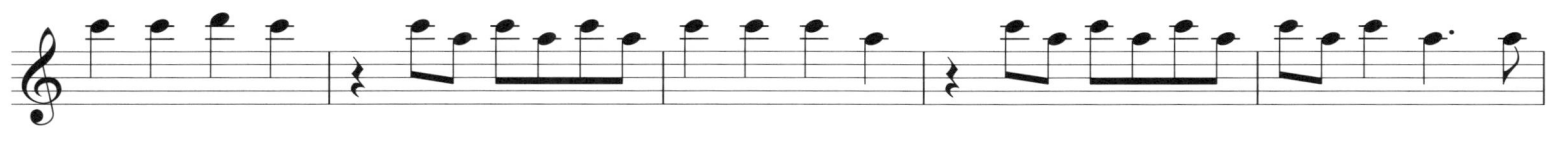

WHEN I WAS YOUR MAN

ALTO SAX

Words and Music by BRUNO MARS,
ARI LEVINE, PHILIP LAWRENCE
and ANDREW WYATT

Slowly, with feeling

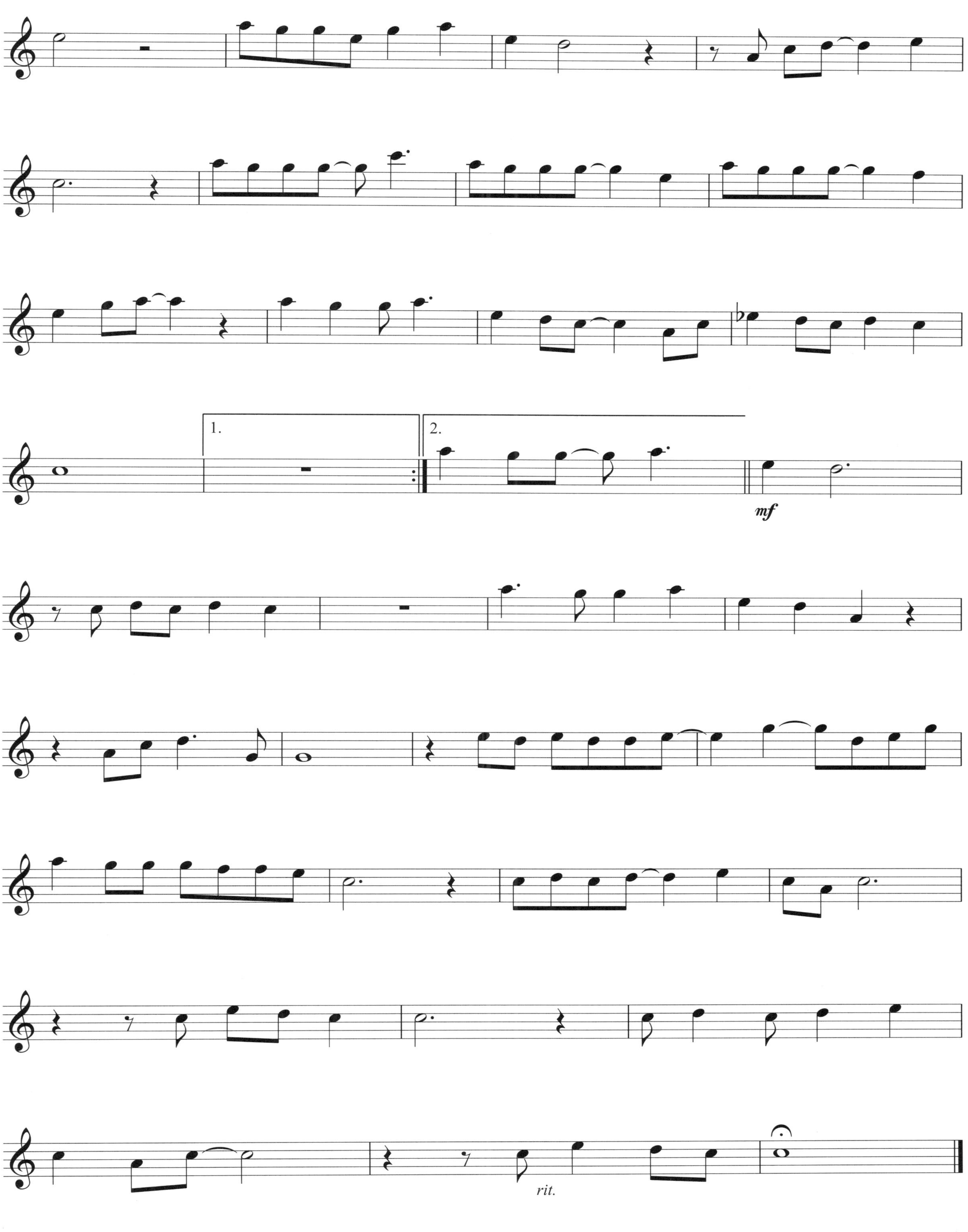
1.
2.
mf
rit.

HAL•LEONARD INSTRUMENTAL PLAY-ALONG

Your favorite songs are arranged just for solo instrumentalists with this outstanding series. Each book includes a great full-accompaniment play-along CD so you can sound just like a pro! Check out **www.halleonard.com** to see all the titles available.

Disney Greats

Arabian Nights • Hawaiian Roller Coaster Ride • It's a Small World • Look Through My Eyes • Yo Ho (A Pirate's Life for Me) • and more.

____	00841934	Flute	$12.95
____	00841935	Clarinet	$12.95
____	00841936	Alto Sax	$12.95
____	00841937	Tenor Sax	$12.95
____	00841938	Trumpet	$12.95
____	00841939	Horn	$12.95
____	00841940	Trombone	$12.95
____	00841941	Violin	$12.95
____	00841942	Viola	$12.95
____	00841943	Cello	$12.95
____	00842078	Oboe	$12.95

Glee

And I Am Telling You I'm Not Going • Defying Gravity • Don't Stop Believin' • Keep Holding On • Lean on Me • No Air • Sweet Caroline • True Colors • and more.

____	00842479	Flute	$12.99
____	00842480	Clarinet	$12.99
____	00842481	Alto Sax	$12.99
____	00842482	Tenor Sax	$12.99
____	00842483	Trumpet	$12.99
____	00842484	Horn	$12.99
____	00842485	Trombone	$12.99
____	00842486	Violin	$12.99
____	00842487	Viola	$12.99
____	00842488	Cello	$12.99

Motown Classics

ABC • Endless Love • I Just Called to Say I Love You • My Girl • The Tracks of My Tears • What's Going On • You've Really Got a Hold on Me • and more.

____	00842572	Flute	$12.99
____	00842573	Clarinet	$12.99
____	00842574	Alto Saxophone	$12.99
____	00842575	Tenor Saxophone	$12.99
____	00842576	Trumpet	$12.99
____	00842577	Horn	$12.99
____	00842578	Trombone	$12.99
____	00842579	Violin	$12.99
____	00842580	Viola	$12.99
____	00842581	Cello	$12.99

Popular Hits

Breakeven • Fireflies • Halo • Hey, Soul Sister • I Gotta Feeling • I'm Yours • Need You Now • Poker Face • Viva La Vida • You Belong with Me • and more.

____	00842511	Flute	$12.99
____	00842512	Clarinet	$12.99
____	00842513	Alto Sax	$12.99
____	00842514	Tenor Sax	$12.99
____	00842515	Trumpet	$12.99
____	00842516	Horn	$12.99
____	00842517	Trombone	$12.99
____	00842518	Violin	$12.99
____	00842519	Viola	$12.99
____	00842520	Cello	$12.99

Sports Rock

Another One Bites the Dust • Centerfold • Crazy Train • Get Down Tonight • Let's Get It Started • Shout • The Way You Move • and more.

____	00842326	Flute	$12.99
____	00842327	Clarinet	$12.99
____	00842328	Alto Sax	$12.99
____	00842329	Tenor Sax	$12.99
____	00842330	Trumpet	$12.99
____	00842331	Horn	$12.99
____	00842332	Trombone	$12.99
____	00842333	Violin	$12.99
____	00842334	Viola	$12.99
____	00842335	Cello	$12.99

Women of Pop

Bad Romance • Jar of Hearts • Mean • My Life Would Suck Without You • Our Song • Rolling in the Deep • Single Ladies (Put a Ring on It) • Teenage Dream • and more.

____	00842650	Flute	$12.99
____	00842651	Clarinet	$12.99
____	00842652	Alto Sax	$12.99
____	00842653	Tenor Sax	$12.99
____	00842654	Trumpet	$12.99
____	00842655	Horn	$12.99
____	00842656	Trombone	$12.99
____	00842657	Violin	$12.99
____	00842658	Viola	$12.99
____	00842659	Cello	$12.99

Twilight

Bella's Lullaby • Decode • Eyes on Fire • Full Moon • Go All the Way (Into the Twilight) • Leave Out All the Rest • Spotlight (Twilight Remix) • Supermassive Black Hole • Tremble for My Beloved.

____	00842406	Flute	$12.99
____	00842407	Clarinet	$12.99
____	00842408	Alto Sax	$12.99
____	00842409	Tenor Sax	$12.99
____	00842410	Trumpet	$12.99
____	00842411	Horn	$12.99
____	00842412	Trombone	$12.99
____	00842413	Violin	$12.99
____	00842414	Viola	$12.99
____	00842415	Cello	$12.99

Twilight – New Moon

Almost a Kiss • Dreamcatcher • Edward Leaves • I Need You • Memories of Edward • New Moon • Possibility • Roslyn • Satellite Heart • and more.

____	00842458	Flute	$12.99
____	00842459	Clarinet	$12.99
____	00842460	Alto Sax	$12.99
____	00842461	Tenor Sax	$12.99
____	00842462	Trumpet	$12.99
____	00842463	Horn	$12.99
____	00842464	Trombone	$12.99
____	00842465	Violin	$12.99
____	00842466	Viola	$12.99
____	00842467	Cello	$12.99

Wicked

As Long As You're Mine • Dancing Through Life • Defying Gravity • For Good • I'm Not That Girl • Popular • The Wizard and I • and more.

____	00842236	Book/CD Pack	$11.95
____	00842237	Book/CD Pack	$11.95
____	00842238	Alto Saxophone	$11.95
____	00842239	Tenor Saxophone	$11.95
____	00842240	Trumpet	$11.95
____	00842241	Horn	$11.95
____	00842242	Trombone	$11.95
____	00842243	Violin	$11.95
____	00842244	Viola	$11.95
____	00842245	Cello	$11.95

FOR MORE INFORMATION, SEE YOUR LOCAL MUSIC DEALER, OR WRITE TO:

HAL•LEONARD® CORPORATION
7777 W. BLUEMOUND RD. P.O. BOX 13819 MILWAUKEE, WI 53213